Published by Glenn
45 Julian Rɩ
West Bridgfᴜ.ᴜ
Nottingham
NG2 5AJ, U.K.
Quality paperback copies US$15.00 or UK£10.00,
Delivered free worldwide from glennfhill@aol.com

First published in Great Britain 2008
Fifth Edition 2018
Copyright © Glenn Francis Hill 2018

Glenn Francis Hill asserts the moral right to be
identified as the author of this work.
ISBN 978-0-9560052-2-9

Printed and bound in Great Britain by
Prime Group Limited
Unit 8, Burma Road, Blidworth,
Notts. NG21 0RT, U.K.

Glenn F. Hill
45 Julian Rd., W. Bridgford
Nottingham NG2 5AJ
Tel: 0115-982-2546
e-mail: glennfhill@aol.com

ACKNOWLEDGEMENTS

Grateful thanks to my daughters Jennifer and Sarah for advice on word processing and page layout and to my wife Lorna for proof reading the manuscript.

My thanks also to Harry Horsley and Brian Turley for their encouragement.

DEDICATION

This book is dedicated to the memory of Thomas Aikenhead, aged 18, a theology student at Edinburgh University in 1696. He was found guilty of blasphemy and hanged at Edinburgh on the 8th January 1697. All he did was speak the truth.

The design of the front cover of this booklet is inspired by the cover of the 1794 first English edition of *The Age of Reason* by Thomas Paine (1737-1809).

CONTENTS

RELIGION EXPLAINED
IN AN HOUR

Analysis of Faith
by Glenn Francis Hill

There are over six billion people in the world, every one of them has heard of religion, tens of thousands have died because of it, few try to explain it.

"Humanity's greatest weakness is its tendency to delude itself as to the veracity of unexamined convictions".

John Stuart Mill. (1806-1873)

"The conflict of faith and scepticism remains the proper, the only, the deepest theme of the history of the world and mankind to which all others are subordinate".

Johann Wolfgang von Goethe. (1749-1832).

OPENING

On the afternoon of the 11th of September 2001 I was at my computer writing a letter when the telephone rang. I heard the voice of my son James in a desperate tone say,
"Dad, switch on the TV, Now!"
"What channel?" I asked
The reply was, "Any channel, any channel".
"What's it about?" I asked
He said, "Just do it now, we'll talk about it later, just do it now!"
"OK" I said. Putting the phone down, I galloped downstairs and switched on the television. The scene was unforgettable, the New York skyline, a beautiful bright sunny day, a twin engine airliner suddenly appeared and melted into a massive boxlike tower of the World Trade Centre. I stared in amazement, as a former pilot I could not understand such faulty navigation or such pilot error. While I stared stunned and aghast at the burning building, another twin engine airliner appeared and crashed into the other twin tower. This was no accident! What on earth was happening! It could only be an attack. Within a few hours it was announced that the attack was being exulted in triumph by Islamic terrorists and pictures were shown of Palestinians dancing for joy in the streets of Gaza at the news of the atrocity.

What could be the cause of all this hatred and bitterness?
Until the age of thirteen I had lived in India and gone to school with the children of Muslims and others where there had been no trace of racial or religious animosity. Indeed, my very earliest memory in 1936, before the age of two, is of being carried in the arms of Kabula Khan, my father's elderly cook in Calcutta, he was a Shia Muslim and a grandfather. I used to cling around his neck and kiss his cheek, I still remember the feel of his stubble whiskers. Kabula Khan told me his family came originally from Lucknow, although he must have had Afghan ancestors to be given his name. He taught me my first sentence of human language and my mother and grandmother made such a fuss about it that it remains forever my earliest memory.

Let us look at the causes of the hatred and bitterness that led to the destruction of the World Trade Centre.

"We have just enough religion to make us hate, but not enough to make us love one another",

Jonathan Swift. (1669-1745).

CAUSE AND EFFECT
FROM TURPENTINE TO TWIN TOWERS

In 1915 during the First World War the British Government was in serious trouble due to a shortage of the vital war material cordite, used as the propellant for Artillery shells. The trench warfare stalemate of the Western Front had developed into an enormous and hideous artillery duel in which both sides tried to turn their enemy's front line into an area of overlapping shell craters. In those early days cordite was made using acetone derived from pine oil, previously obtained from the pine forests of Canada or the Baltic countries. The enclosed Baltic Sea was closed to Allied ships and ships from Canada were being sunk by German submarines. Unless this problem could be solved the British Prime Minister David Lloyd George could foresee early defeat. A scientific adviser told Lloyd George that he knew of a Jewish professor of Chemistry, Chaim Weizmann at Manchester University, who could produce acetone for cordite production from other materials by a distillation process. Chaim Weizmann's patented process solved the critical military supply problem.

Weizmann was a Russian scientist who had settled in England in 1904 to pursue his career in chemistry, he had for many years been a dedicated Zionist, an organisation devoted to the creation of a homeland in Palestine for the dispersed and persecuted Jews of the world. After the crisis was over Lloyd George gave Weizmann his grateful thanks on behalf of the British Empire and offered him a knighthood, a peerage, a country estate or whatever in his power to show gratitude. Weizmann accepted none of the offers, he just asked Lloyd George if anything could be done to provide for Jewish settlement in their ancient original homeland of Palestine. Lloyd George encouraged Lord Balfour, a British Government Minister, to action the request. The Balfour Declaration was the result, it was a policy to allow Jewish settlement in Palestine after the war and it was published in November 1917

The Allies finally defeated the Central Powers in November, 1918. Since British Empire forces had driven the Turkish forces out of the area, Palestine was mandated to Britain by the League of Nations and Jewish settlement began. Communal tension led to the Jaffa riots and thereafter the British enacted immigration quotas. An exception was made for Jews with over £1000 in cash or the professionally qualified with £500. In those days the value of a middle class home was about £1000. The growing Jewish migration, buying land and property with money from the huge Jewish National Fund (JNF) of the Diaspora upset the native Arab population. They felt they were being outnumbered and displaced from their own ancestral homeland. This led to a large scale rebellion, referred to as the 1936-1939 Arab uprising against the British administration. In 1936 the unrest forced the UK government to station more British troops in Palestine than there were in the whole sub-continent of the Indian Empire.

In 1945 following the near-extermination of European Jews by the Nazis, the American Jewish community expressed increasingly vocal support for the Zionist movement. The British administration in Palestine found itself hated by both Jews and Arabs as it struggled with the increasing unrest. Thousands of Jews were arrested, many held without trial. Thousands of illegal Jewish immigrants in Palestine were deported to British prison camps in Cyprus including Holocaust survivors, women and children. Jewish terrorists responded with anti-British atrocities, amongst other things, by kidnapping and hanging young British conscript soldiers (1947-48 Civil War).

On 29 November 1947, a U.N. resolution required Britain to allow unrestricted migration into Palestine. With a great sense of relief, the British forces left Palestine on 14 May 1948, although Jews of "fighting age" were still held by the British in Cyprus until March 1949. In May 1948, in accordance with the 1947 UN Partition Plan, the Jewish leader David Ben-Gurion announced the creation of the State of Israel.

Chaim Weizmann later became its first President. Israel was immediately recognised by the United States. Atrocities and massacres caused the displacement of about a million Muslim Arabs from Palestine. The Zionist movement included ideas for the creation of a purely Jewish State without other gentile occupants. Removal of the Muslim citizens who had farmed and lived there for over a thousand years was sometimes referred to as "the redemption of the land". This is as if the 4,000 year old myths of Joshua's Old Testament massacres to clear the way for the arrival of the children of Israel from Egypt were being repeated and justified as "God's Will". These actions led to an Arab-Israeli War that involved Egypt, Syria, Jordan, Lebanon, Iraq, Saudi Arabia, Yemen and Arab volunteers, it lasted until March 1949. During this war, a long planned Ethnic Cleansing of Palestine was carried out by the new Jewish state of Israel. This war, known to Israelis as "The War of Independence", but for Palestinians it will forever be the *Nakba*, the "catastrophe".

By the end of this conflict it had involved one of the largest forced migrations in modern history. About a million Palestinian Muslim people were expelled from their ancient ancestral homes at gunpoint, civilians were massacred and 531 Palestinian villages thus emptied were deliberately destroyed and flattened so that they could never be reoccupied. Hundreds of thousands of destitute refugees were forced into neighbouring Muslim countries that were left with the problem of providing for them. The truth about this mass expulsion was systematically distorted and suppressed by the Israeli State. The prominent Israeli academic and historian Ilan Pappe has meticulously researched this shameful episode with access to recently declassified Israeli archive records. Ilan Pappe is senior lecturer of Political Science at Haifa University and author of the book "The Ethnic Cleansing of Palestine" referred to in the attached bibliography, the book contains details of these atrocities and the archive sources of their records. I found it too horrific and distressing to continuously read the awful particulars of Palestinian prisoners being forced to dig their own mass graves before being murdered and the unbearable repeated accounts of whole village exterminations.

Regarding the Arab population, David Ben-Gurion had told the Jewish Agency Executive in June *1938, "I am for compulsory transfer; I do not see anything immoral in it".*

This racial and religious expulsion of Muslim Palestinians, the continuing injustices and discriminations suffered by them in Israel and the West Bank and the continued US support for Israel has caused the hatred and resentment in the Muslim world. These bitter grievances ultimately led to the terrorist destruction of the WTC Twin Towers in New York on 11 September 2001, and other Muslim terrorist atrocities in Europe followed by the Allied reaction conflicts in Afghanistan and Iraq.

Following the anti-racial crimes of the Nazis, the accused were brought before the Nuremberg Tribunal to face justice; but no International Court has ever been convened to charge the Israelis with their anti-Palestinian atrocities.

The USA used to be regarded as an example to the world for justice, liberty and prosperity. International regard for American justice is no longer what it once was. It used to be understood by Americans that there should be no State punishment without proper legal procedure. One hundred and sixty years earlier during the American Civil War, President Abraham Lincoln established a principle when he ruled, "The American military does not do Cruelty!" This noble policy was generally upheld until undermined by President George W. Bush and Secretary Donald Rumsfeld. Their actions involved the imprisonment of Muslims without trial for years at Guantanamo Bay, and "Water Boarding" tortures. These acts give rise to international opprobrium of the United States and the bitter anger of Muslims.

PREFACE

The nature of World conflict has changed through the ages from the national rivalries and Imperial ambitions that culminated in the horrific wars of the twentieth century. The prospect of mass destruction by atomic, chemical, biological and blinding laser weapons are now so awful that the age of national wars is probably finished. Any rational start of such national conflicts is now unlikely, only a leader believing he is acting upon the "Will of God" or an irrational Dictator may try it. Future conflicts will probably be of guerrilla or terrorist forms arising out of injustices or religious causes.

The aim of this booklet is to reduce religious terrorism by encouraging extremists to re-examine the origins and causes of their beliefs. It would not seem right to focus on Islamic beliefs without giving equal attention to the origins and beliefs of the other religions. An explanation is needed for the many different beliefs, unsupported by proper evidence, that have dominated human minds from the earliest times. A major objective has been to try to explain Religion in an hour of reading time. I have tried to make it easy reading with straight talk. One problem is that of judgement for the number of archive sources of evidence that need to be included. If evidence has too long an explanation it loses impact and even clear meaning can get lost in long sentences and elaborate paragraphs. Numbered notes have been avoided together with references that make the reader flick pages back and forth.

INTRODUCTION

It is easy to understand why early man imagined simple explanations for all he saw around him before scientific knowledge became increasingly available. The mysterious causes of sickness and death, earthquakes and volcanoes, sunrise and set, the night sky, tides, moon phases, the various forms of life on earth, etc. caused early man to invent explanations in the absence of scientific knowledge. It is amazing and strange that in these times when scientific knowledge supported by evidence is available some religious believers should still bow down, kneel, worship, praise, beg forgiveness and plead for benefits from a God who was invented and imagined by other men in the very distant past. Puzzling factors of human psychology allow this to happen. Our human thought processes need to be examined when trying to explain the contradictions between the many religious beliefs and the scientific facts of reality.

Some ideas in this booklet are inspired by my childhood experience in the 1940s at the boy's boarding school of St. Paul's School, Darjeeling, India. The school was the property of the Anglican Church. All pupils had to attend Church Services twice a day and three times on Sundays as well as Christian "Divinity" lessons given by Dr Fosse-Westcott, Doctor of Divinity, retired Metropolitan Bishop of India. Most of the three hundred pupils were the children of Hindus, the remainder were children of Christians, Muslims, Sikhs, Buddhists and Jews. It was a puzzle for me to understand why there should be so many contradictory explanations for the realities of existence. Thankfully, as a result of all the exposure to Anglican ritual we boys showed almost no religious interest in our spare time. I can recall only one memorable schoolboy conversation on the subject of religion. It went as follows:-

9

I was once asked by a classmate, "Do you believe in One God?"

I gave my correctly trained answer, "Yes!"

Next question, "Do you believe He is Almighty God with unlimited Power?"

Again my correctly trained answer, "Yes!"

Final question, "If Almighty God chooses to appear as Vishnu, Shiva or Krishna can anything stop Him?"

I shrugged my shoulders and walked away but it was clear to me that, for believers, the idea of One God monotheism had just been utterly trounced by a twelve year old boy. Two or three decades later, I learned that this same irrefutable logic had been used by Guru Nanak, founder of the Sikh faith, when he sought to reconcile Hinduism and Islam.

As a teenager I was at school in India during the religious division of the sub-continent into the two huge countries of India and Pakistan. I wondered why there should have been such terrible atrocities between Muslims and Hindus in the Punjab and Bengal. There had been no trace of religious animosity at the school, only the names of pupils gave clues to their parents' religions.

It is obvious to me now that the opinions of rational thinkers find truth through the understanding of reality based on evidence. All Miracles, Gods, Goddesses, prayers, blessings, curses, spirits, ghosts, angels, witchcraft, sorcery, astrology, tarot cards, forecasting the future by examination of the entrails of sacrificial animals, alien abductions, so called paranormal phenomena and the like have no connection at all with the realities of existence. For example, the huge Christian sect of the Mormons believe that their sacred text was dictated in an ancient forgotten language onto gold plates by the angel Moroni, buried near Palmyra, New York, U.S.A. and subsequently dug up by Joseph Smith in 1827 who then translated them by burying his face into a hat containing magic stones. According to Smith, the gold plates of evidence were then taken back to heaven by the angel Moroni.

Beliefs unsupported by evidence have caused the atrocities of the Crusades and the Holy Inquisition, the burning or drowning of thousands of "witches", wars and murders between Catholics and Protestants in Europe, Tsarist pogroms on Jews in Russia, Turks on Armenians, Christians on Muslims in the Balkans, Hindus and Muslims in Kashmir, Jews and Muslims in Palestine, Sunnis and Shias in Iraq to name but a few. Other beliefs unsupported by evidence have been behind the atrocities of the Nazis and others. Psychiatrists studying the accused at the 1946 Nuremberg War Crimes Tribunal concluded that those convicted had in common a general state of mind in which individual moral conscience had been abandoned and replaced by faith in Hitler's Nazi Party beliefs.

WHAT IS RELIGION?

Those who can imagine the existence of such powers, called God or Gods, imagine they can influence them to act in their favour. By means of prayers, incantations or rituals, deluded believers are comforted by hope and expectation of special treatment and favours from imaginary supernatural powers.

"Religion is the Opiate of the People". This idea originates as a phrase in Karl Marx's *Introduction to a critique of Hegel's Philosophy of Law.* Marx (1818-1883), was a scholar and philosopher whose ideas had profound effects on the world of the twentieth century. Marx's ideas to promote equality and reduce poverty produced unintended consequences. His publications, *The Communist Manifesto* and *Das Capital* led to totalitarian Communist regimes that ultimately were unable to compete economically with free market economies. Most Communist regimes became so restrictive that their borders were made prison-like to prevent their people voting with their feet and escaping to the liberty and prosperity of happier lands. Worst of all, East-West confrontation during the "Cuban Missile Crisis" of October1962 almost led to a thermonuclear rocket exchange of "Mutually Assured Destruction" or "MAD" that would have returned civilisation to the Stone Age. The world was saved by a heroic Soviet submariner Vasili Arkhipov who circumvented an order to launch a nuclear torpedo.

The relevant paragraph by Marx on religion is copied below.
"Religion is the sigh of the oppressed creature, the kindliness of a heartless world, the soul of soulless circumstance. Religion is the opiate (opium drug) of the people. The removal of religion as the illusory happiness of the people is the demand for its real happiness. The demand that it should give up illusions about its real conditions is the demand that it should give up the conditions which make illusions necessary"

WHAT IS FAITH?

"FAITH IS FAITH IN SOMEONE ELSE'S FAITH"

This undeniable truth comes from "*The Will to Believe*" by the American philosopher William James (1842-1910)

Religious Faith is merely unshakable trust that another person's profoundly irrational beliefs are absolutely true.

It is in this way that weird reports of unbelievable supernatural stories get passed on by very gullible people as absolute truth throughout hundreds of generations for thousands of years.

Some students without any previous religious beliefs choose to study religion because it is the easy career option. Any rational person who has studied religious theology for two or three years must realise that these old supernatural stories of ancient superstitions are all founded on imaginary nonsense.

Some employees of religions start with faith but lose it later. Some of the highest paid find salary less important than being respectfully treated. A few have the opportunity as bishops to posture about in expensive robes and fancy dress pointy hats. In cathedrals they can then enjoy the adulation of faithful congregations. There are some members of congregations who are unable to think for themselves and thus feel a need to find and submit to someone whom they hope will be a wise and knowledgeable adviser who will tell them what to believe.

Many employees of religions, devoid of any faith, repeat old beliefs in order to hold onto high status, salaries and pensions.

WHY IS THERE RELIGIOUS BELIEF?

THE VITAL ANSWER

The innocent impressionable minds of children are imprinted with ideas from adults who tell them that impossible supernatural stories of the distant past truly happened. In this way beliefs can become unshakably imprinted upon young minds.

Everyone, without exception, begins life as small, weak, innocent and ignorant infants and children who are looked after by bigger, stronger and more experienced adults. It is adults who provide love, comfort, security and who take responsibility for everything. This leaves the subconscious impression on some immature adult minds that they are somehow still looked after and even punished by a wise and all powerful parent figure, i.e. GOD.

HOW DO BELIEFS ENTER THE MIND?

Ideas in general and beliefs in particular pass freely by listening or reading from one person's mind into another's mind. This happens in rather the same way that medical infections are passed from body to body, the difference is that many ideas are beneficial.

Spinoza (1632-1677) the Dutch Jewish rationalist philosopher suggested that as soon as one comprehends a new idea, one immediately believes, after which secondary thoughts quickly arise to check out the belief to understand whether it is true or false. (Is it meant as a joke? Is it fact or fiction? Does it make sense? Is the speaker trustworthy? And so on). In a few people these secondary thought impulses are absent or only weakly experienced. Spinoza had deduced an explanation of animal behaviour that was to be confirmed by zoologists 300 years later. It was discovered that hatching goslings were convinced that the first moving creature they saw was their parent and they would thereafter slavishly follow a dog, pig or human, unable to shake off this enduring mental imprint. Similarly many humans become imprinted with the first religious ideas they receive as children and become convinced that they are unshakable truths. Thereafter, like goslings, they are often unable to seriously consider other possibilities.

THE NATURE OF BELIEF

Our present world is threatened by a few religious fanatics whose minds are filled with hatred based on extraordinary beliefs. These are people who would destroy whole portions of civilisation if only they could get their hands on deadly atomic, chemical, or biological weapons. A solution to this problem would be to persuade those religious fanatics to reconsider the truth of their beliefs. Everything one learns about the motivations of religious terrorists confirms an opinion of Voltaire (1694-1778), man of letters and philosopher. He was hailed as the greatest French champion of the Enlightenment and his generation's most courageous spokesman for freedom and toleration.

Voltaire famously wrote,
"Those who can make you believe absurdities can make you commit atrocities".

The great difficulty in persuading fanatics of the absurdity or implausibility of their beliefs is a factor of human nature that almost prevents such unwise fanatics from hearing explanations or even listening to other ideas, let alone entering into conversational dialogue about their beliefs.

Ibn Rushd (1126-1198), also known in Europe as Averroes, the great Muslim philosopher of twelfth century Cordoba encountered this problem. He said that mankind was divided into two groups comprising:-

Firstly, a wise minority of those who could discuss any subject and maintain a calm academic tone throughout.

Secondly, the unwise majority, in his day the illiterate masses, of those who just got angry, confused or upset when they heard the plausibility of their opinions being questioned.

Socrates (469-399BC), a philosopher of ancient Athens, developed a question and answer system for examining the plausibility and truth of opinions. It has become known as the "Socratic Method", his system uncovers truth by exposing faulty reasoning behind some ideas. The schoolboy conversation at St. Paul's, Darjeeling, on page 10 above, is a good example of the Socratic Method. When Socrates applied his method to the subject of religion in ancient Athens he got into serious trouble with the city's elected rulers. He was charged with denying religion and corrupting the city's youth with impious ideas.

FREE SPEECH AND COERCION

- Spinoza was charged with heretical thought at Amsterdam in 1656.

- Voltaire had to flee France for his views on liberty.

- Ibn Rushd was banished to Morocco for questioning Islamic opinions.

- Socrates was condemned to commit suicide by drinking hemlock.

"Whoever knew Truth put to the worse in a free and open encounter"
John Milton (1608-1674).

CAUSES OF IRRATIONAL BELIEF

There are many causes why some people hold beliefs that are not supported by logic, reasoning or evidence. One important cause and thirteen other numbered random examples follow below.

Honest decent trusting people who would never knowingly deceive or mislead others naturally trust and believe others. This is the most important cause of the acceptance of irrational beliefs because this category includes all children. This cause is therefore more important than the total of all those other factors listed below. Thomas B. Czerner, M.D., Clinical Professor of Ophthalmology at the University of the California School of Medicine in San Francisco writes, "*It is in the first years of life that the most profound imprints of experience are stamped on the brain*".

Supernatural religious ideas have been imprinted on the minds of children for centuries with disastrous effects in parts of the world. These religious notions include ideas about biologically impossible virgin birth, a zoologically impossible winged flying horse (Buraq), and chemically impossible alcohol production without fermentation (water into wine), medically impossible sudden cures (miracles), astronomically and geologically impossible locations (Heaven & Hell) and other such ideas.

A few examples of other factors causing some people's irrational beliefs are listed below:-

1.   Checking whether an existing opinion is true or false requires too much investigative effort.

2.   Reality is so uncomfortable that more comforting beliefs are preferred.

3.   Many of the things seen around them have been made by someone so they assume the entire Universe must have been made by someone.

4.   If they admit that they do not believe they fear that they will lose friends at their Church or Mosque, Synagogue, Mormon Temple, Masonic Lodge or whatever other social group.

5.   If they are Muslims and admit disbelief they fear they may be stoned to death under Islamic Law.

6.   They think their beliefs must be true because many others around say they are true. This is a "Chicken with Crust Effect" that sometimes affects stock market traders, Bank Runs and passing fads. The flock is feeding on plenty of grain scattered on a farmyard. One chicken finds a crust and runs with it; all others then stop feeding and chase the one with the crust.

7.   The "Dr. Goebbels Effect", Propaganda, however false, if repeated emphatically will be believed by most people who continue to listen.

8.   The "Werther's Effect". In 1774 Johann Wolfgang von Goethe, the great German philosopher, poet and author published his successful novel, "Leiden des jungen Werthers" – "Sorrows of Young Werther". It is the tragedy of a suicidal lovesick youth. Its publication was followed by so many suicides of young men in German speaking Europe that the book was banned by governments. Similarly, some emotional appeals of religion can induce others to follow instinctively.

9.   If they admit that they do not believe in the leadership of Stalin or Hitler, Saddam Hussein, Pol Pot or other tyrant they fear execution by State Authorities.

10.   In the past it was true to say, "If they did not believe church teaching they would be tortured by the Church Authorities".

11.   If they do not believe in God they do believe God will burn them in Hell forever, (A strange paradox).

12.   In the Middle East some attitudes prevail that go as follows in questioning beliefs. "My parents told me these beliefs are true! You cast doubt on them! You are calling my family liars or fools! Honour demands vengeance for your insult!" This is a classic example of Ibn Rushd's opinion of the unwise majority. The reaction is angry and upset, the philosophical notions of the new ideas offered are not considered in a calm academic state of mind. There are similarities to the "Chicken with Crust Effect" since the new ideas lie scattered and only the vengeful notion is blindly pursued.

13.   There were historical times in Europe when it was mortally dangerous for any Christian to admit disbelief. These were difficult times for philosophers to talk or write freely. Blaise Pascal (1623-1662) the French mathematician, physicist and philosopher suggested the following. It became known as, "Pascal's Wager". He suggested that the "best bet" was to believe in God. If God existed then the prospect of eternal bliss in heaven was clearly better than the alternative of eternal torture in hell. However, he reasoned, if God did not exist it would not matter either way because neither eternal bliss nor eternal torture would then exist.

DEAD RELIGIONS OF THE PAST

Examples of the dead religions of the past include those of ancient Egypt, Greece, Rome, Persia (Iran), Palestine, Carthage (now in Tunisia), Babylon (now in Iraq), Assyria (now Syria), Scandinavia, Mexico and Peru. However, sufficient historical archive information remains for us to get a good idea of some of their many strange beliefs.

The ancient Egyptians created impressive buildings and works of art. Their religion incorporated belief in many gods including part animal, part human examples. In 1799 the Rosetta stone was discovered in Egypt. Its inscription is copied in the three languages of Hieroglyphic, Demotic and Greek, enabling the mysterious and extensive ancient Egyptian hieroglyphic inscriptions to be translated into modern languages at last. These tell about the spirit of the god Osiris entering the virgin goddess Isis to produce the god Horus and the resurrection of the dead god Osiris to judge the souls of the dead of mankind. These original very ancient Egyptian ideas must surely be the source of their later use in Judaism, Christianity and Islam.

The ancient Greeks and Romans believed in many gods, often the same gods with different names in their own languages, Zeus of the Greeks and Jupiter of the Romans being their names for the father of the gods. Aphrodite of the Greeks is Venus of the Romans being the goddess of love and so on. There was an assumption of the supernatural idea in these religions that it was possible to influence the power of the gods by promising prayers, gifts or sacrifices in the hope that requests to the gods would be granted.

The related ancient Philistines, Phoenicians and Carthaginians believed in about eighteen different gods and goddesses including gods of war, sun, moon, fertility, craftsmanship, healing, fire, death, dawn, dusk, plague, chaos, agriculture and the like. Their religion included practices involving parents burying their children who had been sacrificed to the gods.

The political crisis at Carthage in 310 B.C. resulted in five hundred children being sacrificed, killed and burnt and recent archaeological excavations have revealed great numbers of children's bones in funerary urns at the site.

The ancient Babylonians and Assyrians also believed in numerous gods with different names but similar supposed functions of responsibility for heaven, weather, wisdom, writing, love, war, etc. There seemed to be an assumption in these ancient religions that it was presumed or hoped that if the worshippers made some wasteful sacrifice by burning food or pouring wine away as offering to the gods that the gods may then respond by granting wishes.

The ancient Scandinavian and Germanic peoples also believed in several gods, Odin king of the gods, Thor god of thunder, Loki god of cunning, Hel goddess of the underworld and several lesser gods. It is wearisome to keep listing details of the many dead religions of the past but it serves to illustrate the weird and sometimes thoroughly nasty ideas that some religions can use.

The Incas, Mayas and Aztecs of the New World had religions that involved worship of sun, moon, rain, corn, lightening, etc. These religions incorporated animal and human sacrifices; the Incas whose king was regarded as the sun god required 200 children to be sacrificed at his enthronement. The Mayan faith used divination, astrology, bloodletting, torture and human sacrifices. The Aztecs sacrificed children to their rain god for crops and sacrificed adults to the sun god to ensure daily sunrise.

Ancient Persian's Zoroastrian beliefs encompassed a collection of Gods, Ahura Mazda who created and sustained of the universe, Mitra who protected truth and contracts, Anhita the war goddess, Rashu god of justice and astral deities such as Tishtria. The vast civilisation of the Persian empire of around 500BC extended from the shores of the Mediterranean in the west to the banks of the Indus River in India in the east. Mithras, a development of the Persian God Mitra was adopted by Roman Legionaries whose shrines have been found as far northwest as Hadrian's Wall on the borders of Scotland. The cult of Mithras was at one time a serious rival to Christianity in its early years. Zoroastrian beliefs remain on a comparatively very small scale, held by the Parsees of India and in some remote villages in Iran.

Religions that are practised today include beliefs that are just as strange as those of the dead religions of the past, but without so much sacrifice.

There exist the religions of present worshippers and historical records of the dead religions of the past. When a religion has no more worshippers or followers it is dead and so are its imaginary gods or god. Archive record copies and ancient accounts of some dead religions remain in existence but without any remaining worshippers these religions of the past have no significance except as historical novelties. However, some ideas from the dead religions of the past have persisted into present religions. Over centuries of time religions have come into existence and have finally gone forever. As people became better educated and more rational, the similar Flat Earth religious beliefs with Gods above clouds and Hell below a flat world have also ended.

Ultimately, at some time in the future, the irrational religions of the present will assuredly die out in the same way and join the long list of the dead religions of the past.

RELIGIOUS FUNDAMENTALISM

Religious fundamentalism is an attitude of mind rather than an idea. It is most commonly found as a matter of opinions relating to the inspirations of the "holy" books of the Jews, the Christians and the Muslims. Fundamentalist believers of these faiths accept the divine authorship of every sentence of these scriptures. It should be explained that the fundamentalist believers of each of these three religions hold that the scripture of their own faith is absolutely true as the words of God and the other two scriptures contain parts that are either false or mistaken. To Fundamentalists, the Old Testament of the Bible of the Jews, The New Testament of the Christians and the Koran of the Muslims are regarded as the mouth piece of God and their authors are no more responsible for content than a computer keyboard would be to an author of novels.

Fundamentalists cannot accept assumptions of criticism of these scriptures. They cannot consider that these scriptures even in part are human documents that can be studied like other human documents. For a fundamentalist to admit this would be tantamount to giving up the faith. If apparent discrepancies are pointed out, or manuscript difficulties are shown, it is regarded as an illusion of the Devil. In the nineteenth century, fundamentalists explained away fossils and the antiquity of the earth. Fundamentalists maintain that their scriptures are as easy as they are truthful and require no aids. This is a position belonging to the nineteenth century. Similar opinions can be found among simple people in earlier periods, but mainly when knowledge of natural science was slight or confined to a few. Even in the Middle Ages a more critical attitude could be found wherever there were scholars to cope with it.

In the eighteenth century the new physics hardened into a "scientific ideology" – the mechanistic deism of the Enlightenment. On this view God was kicked upstairs to the lonely dignity of First Cause and the Great Architect of the Universe. Once begun, this idea held that the universe must run along precisely determined lines to an exactly calculable time-table. This concept meant that God could not intervene in human affairs, so there was no place for revelation and little interest in the Bible amongst Christian intellectuals. A few generations later, when this was added to the evidence of evolution, it seemed to many honest minds that Scripture was utterly discredited.

Some could not accept this but would not argue for an alternative: some placed their faith above their integrity and the characteristically nineteenth- century form of fundamentalism was created, an impregnable mountain of sand in which the intellectually feeble could comfortably bury their heads.

Fundamentalism has recently impacted strongly into American religious thought. As late as 1925 a schoolteacher in Tennessee was put on trial for teaching Evolution in a school. He was found guilty though no measures were taken. Fundamentalism remains a strong undercurrent.

In the final analysis, fundamentalist believers have saved themselves the trouble of ever having to think for themselves. They choose to avoid the effort of applying reasoning or logic to their own thoughts. They are simply enslaved by some ideas that they have allowed to become imprinted in their brains.

Religious fundamentalists are drawn to comforting beliefs that are easily acquired and remain unquestioned thereafter.

HALLUCINATION PSYCHOSES

Psychosis was first used in 1845 as an alternative word to insanity or mania by Ernst von Feuchtersleben, (1806-1849), the Austrian philosopher and physician who was dean of the faculty of medicine at the University of Vienna. The word Psychosis stems from the Greek *Psyche* (soul) and *–osis* (diseased or subnormal condition).

The well known clinical medical illness called hallucination psychosis is a vital factor for understanding of the origins of the three Middle Eastern religions of Judaism, Christianity and Islam and for understanding the psychotic mental states suffered by their founders. This mental state, so well known to doctors, psychologists and psychiatrists is often described as a "loss of contact with reality".

A wide variety of stressors, both organic and functional can cause such psychotic reactions (forty days and nights in the wilderness?) Many psychotic patients experience visions, unseen by others, referred to as visual hallucination, and some sufferers experience voices in their heads unheard by others around them. Those who have had some knowledge of religions sometimes ascribe these delusions to the voice of God, Angels or the Devil. Psychiatrists encounter many patients who claim to hear the Devil speaking to them or even urging them to evil or violent acts. There are other patients who claim to hear the voice of God and they sometimes experience Delusions of Grandeur as a result.

Hallucinations are defined by the authorities of mental illness as sensory perception in the absence of external stimuli. They are different from illusions, or perceptual distortions, which are the misrepresentations of external stimuli. Hallucinations may occur in any of the five senses and take almost any form. This booklet is concerned here with reference to religion and therefore applies to the specific cases of the heard and seen hallucinations experienced by Abraham, Jesus Christ and Muhammad.

26

Karl Theodor Jaspers (1883-1969), the great German psychiatrist and professor of philosophy at Heidelberg University, classified psychotic delusions into *primary* and *secondary* types.

Primary delusions are defined as arising out of the blue and not being comprehensible in terms of normal mental processes, whereas secondary delusions may be understood as being influenced by the person's background or current situation, including for example religious or superstitious beliefs. In some examples of these psychoses the sufferers may be completely unaware that their vivid hallucinations and impossible delusions are in any way unrealistic.

Hallucinatory psychoses are sometimes a factor of manic depressive insanity (now called bipolar disorder) and sometimes a factor of dementia praecox (now called schizophrenia).

In world terms the effect of mass belief in the psychotic hallucinations of the founders of Judaism, Christianity and Islam has been profound. It has led to dreadful conflicts and violence.

THE SIX MAJOR WORLD RELIGIONS

Before describing the six major world religions it is necessary to explain why the great philosophies of China and Japan are not included in the list of major world religions. These two philosophies are concerned with essential human duty to goodness for peace, happiness and order in society. They do not embrace "Belief in a superhuman controlling power" and so they cannot be defined as religions in accordance with this Oxford Dictionary definition.

The Confucian philosophy of China was propounded by K'ung fu-tzu, (551-479BC) meaning in Chinese *Venerable Master Kung* and known in European languages as Confucius. His philosophy is recorded in the "Analects" which are a collection of notes. Briefly, it embraces the following general ideas:

- Human-heartedness (Ren or jen) is regarded as the highest virtue and the ultimate goal of education.
- The path to Ren is in the practice of social norms (which can change).
- The principle governing social norms involves the personal individual development of proper character and rationality.
- Education of the individual is preparation for a peaceful and orderly society.
- The conduct of the rulers of society should be a good example to the people.
- To govern a disorderly society, the rulers must reintroduce the social norms.

The Shinto customs and rituals of Japan have no known founder and have no single philosophical scripture. These are their general ideas:

- Shinto is wholly devoted to life in this world and it emphasises man's essential duty to goodness. Shinto recognises no split between our natural physical world and the imaginary or transcendental. The worldly and the otherworldly are regarded as a unified entity.
- Shinto worship is carried out in homes or at shrines, it is highly ritualised, it is focused on respect for others, respect for nature and respect for the Emperor who was regarded as a living god.
- Shinto rituals can express wishes for good fortune in the future or the sentiment of thanks for past experience of good fortune.
- Shinto customs are sometimes mixed with the customs of the Buddhist religion that are described later.

It seems strange to be able to count only six major religions in the world, although each of these six has minor subdivisions around the basic beliefs.

Ranked in order of their nominal numbers and world percentages these are:-

Christians, (Christianity)   2.4 billion, 33.00%

Muslims, (Islam)   1.8 billion, 24.10%

Hindus, (Hinduism)   1.15 billion, 15.00%

Buddhists, (Buddhism)   521 million, 7.00%

Sikhs, (Sikhism)   30 million, 0.32%

Jews, (Judaism)   14 million, 0.20%

The present major religions of the world can be divided into two very different categories. Three similar and associated intolerant religions are based on so called "revelations" and originated in the Middle East. They are Judaism, Christianity and Islam, each of these three religions originated in the minds of three individual Founders who heard "Voices in their Heads".

This audible hallucination is a symptom of serious personality disorder recognised by established medical science. It is accepted by world medical authorities and is described in innumerable medical papers and books including Dr. Richard Bentall's book "Madness Explained" and in the Oxford Dictionary of Psychology. The personal accounts of these three founders record their psychotic experiences of hearing disembodied voices in their heads and of having conversations with and even visual hallucinations of imaginary entities.

The other three religions Hinduism, Buddhism and Sikhism originated in India and arose out of meditation, philosophy and ancient traditional stories. There is a great difference between the three Middle Eastern religions and the three religions of Indian origin. The Middle Eastern Jehovah or Allah based group incorporates ancient laws with severe punishments for failure to believe. The three tolerant religions of Indian origin have no such punishment ideas for failure to believe.

.

THE THREE RELIGIONS OF
THE MIDDLE EAST

Each religion is described here by a short summary of its founding origins followed by a brief note on its beliefs. Jews, Christians and Muslims all claim to worship the same God. Judaism was established first and Christianity became a development or heresy of Judaism. Islam was a development that followed both Judaism and Christianity. Judaism will therefore be dealt with first followed by Christianity then Islam, so that each will be in its historical order.

Before describing the origins and beliefs of these three religions of Middle Eastern origin one should again consider modern psychiatric knowledge concerning the hallucinatory symptom of hearing voices in the head. This condition is now recognised as a Personality Disorder suffered in forms of depression, manic depression or schizophrenia. These forms of madness were symptoms suffered by Abraham, Jesus and Muhammad, the founders of the Middle Eastern religions of Judaism, Christianity and Islam. Their personalities and mental disabilities explain the incredibility of their ideas. Disembodied voice hallucinatory symptoms of Personality Disorder are also experienced by some criminally insane lunatics. These personality disorders can now usually be treated with medicines and psychiatric counselling so effectively that mental asylums have now been almost emptied and reserved for only the most unfortunate sufferers. Anyone who suffers these symptoms nowadays is usually medically diagnosed and given treatment. The other possibility, of course, is that the three founders of these religions were merely charlatans lying that they had been specially chosen and spoken to by an Almighty God. Alternatively, they may have deliberately invented or copied these ideas to get attention and to make themselves appear important.

Two thousand and more years ago Jews who changed their religion were killed by Jewish authorities. Five hundred years ago Christians who changed their religion were killed by Christian authorities. At the present time, in some Islamic countries, Muslims who change their religion may be killed by Islamic authorities.

ETERNAL TORTURE

This is a distinguishing feature of the religions of the Jews, Christians and Muslims. They believe their God continuously tortures billions of souls of unbelievers and "sinners" forever.

Pol Pot's Cambodian prison torturers would hang victims until unconscious, revive them and re-hang them daily, even this is mild compared to the Middle Eastern God's ideas for infidels.

A Jewish example can be found in Deuteronomy 32:24&25 involving "burning with heat and hunger, tearing with the teeth of beasts, poisoning with serpent's stings, etc.", this is to be done to old and young, virgins and even suckling babies.
Christian examples can be found in Matthew 25:41&46 "...cast into everlasting fire for everlasting punishment", and Revelations 20:14&15 has victims thrown into "a lake of fire".

The Muslim Koran has more than 20 verses of cruelty. For example: *"Whoever rejects the faith will be in hell-fire forever" 98:6) ."..garments of fire, boiling water, beaten with iron rods forever" (22:19-22). "..smoke and fire, and made to drink molten brass" (18:29). "..chains, fetters and blazing fire forever" (76:4).*

Religious men in the past invented these cruelties. Some even today justify them in scripture as "God's Will".

Modern doctors would recommend urgent treatment for patients with such sadistic psychopathic symptoms.

THE ORIGINS OF JUDAISM

This religion was begun about 4000 years ago by Abraham who lived in Ur of the Chaldees in Mesopotamia (now Iraq). Abraham said he heard God's voice telling him to lead his followers to Canaan (now Israel/Palestine) and later to make a human sacrifice of his son Isaac, whom he had incestuously fathered on his own half sister (Genesis 20:12). Isaac was tied up by his father and laid on a sacrificial rock, Abraham was about to cut Isaac's throat when heard again the voice directing him to a lamb nearby and to sacrifice it instead.

One wonders what the psychological effect may have been on the in-bred young Isaac, whose mother was also his aunt. This custom of animal sacrifice was continued for centuries thereafter at the old Jewish temple at Jerusalem by priests cutting the throats of doves, lambs and calves to please their God. Muslims still continue to celebrate this event by cutting the throats of sheep, goats or cattle on the date of the annual ritual of Eid-ul-Adha.

Incidentally Abraham's God was a hopeless judge of character in His choice of favourites and angels. Abraham was a liar and a pimp with worse morals than a brothel keeper. Abraham prostituted his wife to the Pharaoh of Egypt lying that she was his sister and afterwards he left Egypt with many riches (Genesis 12:18-20). Later he tried the same lying trick on the king of Gerar (Genesis 20:2-5). This God's choice of Abraham's nephew Lot was no better. Two angels were sent by God to Lot to warn him of impending fire and brimstone whereupon the men of Sodom came to Lot's house to demand that the angels be handed over to be sodomised by them (Genesis 19:5). Lot then made a bargain with the male mob and handed over his two virgin daughters to be gang raped instead and the two cowardly angels did nothing about it (Genesis 19:5).

Later prophets required the stoning to death of those who speak God's name, commit adultery, work on the Sabbath, etc. (Exodus 35:2). Fathers are allowed to sell their daughters into slavery (Exodus 21:7). This is followed by chapters containing more abominations, such as laws for stoning to death those who change their religious beliefs (Deuteronomy 13:6-10) and the massacre of the entire populations of captured towns.

THE SUBJECTION OF WOMEN

Attitudes toward women and girls are shown by the precedents of their sale or barter. Further evils arise out of the custom of genital mutilation known as circumcision (Genesis 17:12). This practice then gives precedence for the horrific custom of female genital mutilation euphemistically referred to as "female circumcision". This awful custom is widespread in North Africa and the Muslim world. It involves surgery, without anaesthetic, for removal of the clitoris and labia minora, so that women cannot have the same pleasures that men enjoy.

Muslim customs in many areas include female genital mutilation. The Prophet Muhammad's nine year old bride is viewed as a precedent for selling young girls into marriage to settle debts or disputes in Afghanistan. The Koran verse that advises modest clothing for women is left open to wide interpretation. For example women have been fined and given ten lashes with a whip for wearing trousers in the Sudan. Islamic law in Pakistan requires rape victims to be whipped for having had illegal sex. (This must surely reduce accusations!).

Under Islamic law wives must obey their husbands, who should beat them if the disobedience continues after they have been admonished, (Koran 4:34). Muslim women are credited with half the intelligence of men and their witness in court is valued at half that of men, (Koran 2:282).

If women are oppressed or left uneducated half of the talent in the society is lost to its civilisation.

THE BELIEFS OF JEWS

The Jews believe that there is only one indivisible God who created the Universe and who is everywhere, invisible, transcendental, omnipresent, above and beyond all earthly things. He is Almighty, Omnipotent, has always existed and will always exist. He is just and merciful. He takes an interest in and listens to each individual. Jews, Christians and Muslims are also paradoxically required at the same time to believe that this same God created man in his own image. Through prophets this God gave laws and customs to be followed together with instructions that His followers must worship Him. In order to be a Jew one's mother must be a Jewess

There are some difficulties for a rational mind to reconcile some attributes of this God, for example:-

- *If God is so Almighty why would He want or need anyone to worship Him?*

- *Does this God's feeble self-confidence need the support of praise from mankind?*

- *If their God is just, the Jews surely cannot have justly deserved the persecutions they suffered for centuries at the hands of Christians culminating in the Nazi Holocaust.*

THE ORIGINS OF CHRISTIANITY

Mary the mother of Jesus Christ was a Jewess so according to Jewish law Jesus was also a Jew. The beginning of Mathew's Gospel gives a genealogy that shows the descent of Mary's husband Joseph from King David of Israel. The purpose of this was to show the lineage of Jesus to fulfil prophesies of the Old Testament that the Messiah would be a descendant of King David. Christians are also paradoxically required to believe at the same time that Jesus was also the child of the adulterous God the Holy Ghost part of God.

According to the Bible Jesus made the following policy statement regarding his method for recruiting of disciples, "If any man come to me and hate not his father, mother, and wife and children, and brethren and sisters, yea and his own life also, he cannot be my disciple" (Luke 14:26). This means his disciples could only be chosen from amongst men who hated all their own families.

Furthermore, Jesus says, "For I am come to set a man at variance against his father, and the daughter against her mother, and the daughter-in-law against her mother-in-law". (Matthew 10:35). The policy of making religious followers abandon their families is also repeated by some Christian fundamentalist sects in America. This practise causes one to wonder what this victim of psychotic hallucinatory disorders was doing leading twelve pathetic social misfits, who hated all their own families, as they wandered unemployed around Palestine during Christ's so called ministry. Have regard to the political situation brewing for the Jewish rebellion against the Roman Empire in Palestine at the time. It is probable that they were funded by rebellious zealots for propaganda purposes to persuade people that the arrival of the prophesied liberating Messiah was imminent. It is also probable that the disciples carried out the function of magician's or conjurer's assistants in the preparation of "miracles" to be performed for public consumption by the illiterate mass of the local population. The full violence of the rebellion broke out in 66AD and it ended in its utter defeat four years later at the horrific siege and destruction of Jerusalem by the Roman legions in 70AD.

Like Abraham, Jesus said he heard voices in his head but also that he had seen the devil and talked with him (Matthew 4:1-10). The earliest Christians were all Jews by birth so at its origin Christianity was a branch of Judaism. The stricter Jews regarded Christians as Jewish heretics and Jesus Christ as the prime heretic for which of course he was later crucified. There is another paradox here, if Jesus had not been crucified there would have been no resurrection and the core distinguishing belief of Christianity would have been missing. The crucifiers therefore did Christians a most important service by making possible belief in resurrection and thereby supposedly giving Christians exclusive access to Heaven. It was only some time after Christ's death that the apostle Paul allowed gentiles (non Jews) to be accepted as Christians. It could thus be said that this later spread of Christianity among gentiles across the world could be called Paulianity. Jews were vilified and persecuted by Christians throughout Europe during the Middle Ages because Christians viewed the death of Christ not as a homicide but as a deicide, believing that Jews had killed their God.

THE BELIEFS OF CHRISTIANS

Jesus Christ introduced his followers to the virtues of compassion and forgiveness, ideas that were not much in vogue in the surrounding pagan Roman world

Christians believe that there is one Almighty God who is divided into three parts, God the Father, God the son (Jesus Christ) and God the Holy Ghost. The chief point at which Christianity differs from Judaism and Islam is in this division of God into three parts together with the Christian belief that only by believing that Christ was crucified dead and arose again can Christian souls go to Heaven after they die. In other words, Christians believe that their God sent His only son to Earth to be whipped, nailed and speared to death so that believers would have Heaven opened to them exclusively. The option for Christians is therefore to believe this or be sent to Hell after death for merciless eternal torture by fire on God's orders.

Christ's death is a variation of the human sacrifice notion that motivated Abraham to prepare to sacrifice his son Isaac. Jesus in this later case is again thought of as a human sacrifice and he is sometimes referred to as "The Lamb of God". Struggle as one might, using high ethical principles or a lofty intellectual approach, it is impossible for a thinking person to make any sense at all out of this strange order supposedly imposed by God upon mankind. An easier understanding of this order from the Christian God to his followers may be gained by seeing it on a base level of criminal extortion. Realise parallels of compulsion between this and, as an example, enforcement by a Mafia Capo on a Sicilian shopkeeper.

"Pay me protection money or your shop will be burnt!"

Whereas, with the Christian God it is simply:-

"Praise Me and believe in Resurrection or you will be burnt!"

40

In the fourth century the Roman Empire of Constantine the Great (c.274-337AD) was disturbed by rioting Christian factions disputing articles of faith. As a result, the Roman Emperor Constantine ordered all Christian bishops to attend a Council at Nicaea in Syria in 325 A.D. Constantine's purpose for the Council meeting was to try to get the bishops to resolve their troublesome doctrinal differences. At this meeting, 250 bishops out of 318 voted for Jesus Christ to be God equal to Almighty God the Father. In those days it was routine for the Roman Senate to elect their Emperor to be a God.

To this day Jesus Christ the Jew is worshipped as God Almighty by Christians because he won a posthumous election to God Almighty by majority vote at the Council of Nicaea in 325 A.D. Had he lost the election to Godhead he would today be regarded as just another Prophet, as he is regarded today by the Muslims and by some Jews.

It is difficult for Christians to consider in a calm academic discourse the possibility that the disciples performed the role of magician's or conjurer's assistants in the preparation of the "miracles". It is similarly difficult for Christians to calmly consider the possibility that the disappearance of Christ's body could have been due to his exhortation to his disciples to drink his blood and eat his flesh (Matt 26:26-27 & Luke 22:19-20) This explanation is mentioned by Lucius Apuleius, the Roman writer of the second century. The ritualised cannibalism called the Mass or Holy Communion is practised by many Christians even to the present day. Alternatively, Christ may have survived or avoided crucifixion, as is believed by Muslims, or his followers may have simply invented resurrection as one more miracle.

It seems that the God of the Jews and Christians was not only a poor judge of character but also suffered the same personality disorders as the founders of those faiths. This same schizophrenic split personality trait appears in the contradictions to be found in the Bible that are listed with chapter and verse details in Burrs, "Self Contradictions of the Bible", published in 1860. Burr presents 144 propositions all perfectly contradicted by their opposites. Jesus' message of loving ones neighbour and turning the other cheek is contradicted by such of his statements as, "If a man abide not in me, he is cast forth as a branch, and is withered; and men gather them and cast them into the fire, and they are burned" (John 15:6) and "Think not that I am come to send peace on earth: I came not to send peace but a sword" (Matthew 10:34).

Burr's list includes the following examples;

"God is seen and heard" / "God is invisible and cannot be heard".

"God is everywhere present, sees and knows all things" / "God is not everywhere present, neither sees nor hears all things".

"God is the author of evil" / "God is not the author of evil".

Adultery is forbidden (in Moses' 10 Commandments) / adultery is allowed (by Abraham).

The father of Joseph, Mary's husband was Jacob / the father of Mary's husband was Heli.

The infant Christ was taken into Egypt / the infant Christ was not taken into Egypt.

John was in prison when Jesus went into Galilee / John was not in prison when Jesus went into Galilee.

Christ is equal with God / Christ is not equal with God.

It is impossible to fall from grace / it is possible to fall from grace.

So it goes on until it becomes wearisome, all supported by reference details from the Old and New Testaments.

The religions of the Jews and Christians are discredited by the behaviour and Personality Disorders of their founders and immediate followers. The histories of these religions reveal the ugly laws of and massacres carried out by the ancient Israelites and the torturing and burning of heretics, Jews, Muslims and "witches" by Christians. As recently as 1922 in England John William Gott was sentenced to nine months hard labour for blasphemy (comparing Jesus to a Circus Clown).

Was God the Father pleased that Mr Gott was jailed for calling his son names?

THE ORIGINS OF ISLAM

The historical information in this section is taken from the Hadiths which are accepted Islamic historical archive sources. It is clear that Muhammad must have been well aware of the particulars of the religions of the Jews and the Christians before he started preaching Islam. Muhammad was born at Mecca in 570AD when the town was occupied by an army of Christian Abyssinians. In 572AD a general revolt against the Abyssinians among the tribes of the Yemen ended their rule over southern Arabia. Fifty years earlier in the 520s the young Dhu Nuwas, King of Himyar in the Yemen had converted to Judaism and threatened to unite all southern Arabia under his charismatic authority. Dhu Nuwas regarded the Christian Arabs of the Yemen as his enemies. He began to purge the region of Christians in 523AD.

Through his contacts with Jews and Christians Muhammad would have had knowledge of the stories about the Archangel Gabriel mentioned in Daniel (8:16 & 9:21) in the Old Testament and Luke (1:19, 26) in the New Testament. Muhammad used the name Gabriel to explain the voice of the messenger he said he heard who had been sent to him by God (Al-Lah means The God in Arabic). More 1,400 year old detail is known about the life and conversations of Muhammad than of any other historical figure of centuries ago. Muhammad was at first unpopular in Mecca because his views threatened the town's original annual pagan pilgrimage earnings. For personal safety reasons Muhammad moved north one night to join a band of his supporters at the oases at Yathrib (later called Medina).

In addition to the voices in his head Muhammad said he flew one night from Mecca to the temple site at Jerusalem on a winged horse named Buraq provided by the Archangel Gabriel. On arrival at the temple he was met by Abraham, Moses and Jesus who were waiting for him. From Jerusalem, remounting Buraq, he flew to Heaven, where he met Adam, Noah, Moses, Abraham and Jesus.

Passing beyond all these until even the Archangel Gabriel dared go no further, he found himself in the presence of Almighty God (Allah). He was allowed a glimpse of Heaven and a glance into the infernal regions of Hell and received detailed orders for prayer rituals. Thence, remounting Buraq, he returned to Mecca in a few minutes.

On another occasion Muhammad flew a return trip to Heaven riding Buraq and had a successful negotiation with Allah about the number of times per day that the faithful should pray to Him, reducing the requirement of prayer from fifty five times per day down to a more practical level of five times per day. Incidentally, a flying animal with the weight of a horse (500kg), which is fifty times the weight of an albatross (10kg and 3m wingspan) would need fifty times its wingspan to fly, i.e. 150m, a longer wingspan than any aircraft.

Originally the Muslims at Medina prayed northwards toward Jerusalem but later Gabriel brought a message for a turnaround and future prayers to be redirected south toward their hometown of Mecca. When Muhammad was aged fifty three he took a third wife named Aisha, she was the nine year old daughter of Abu Bekr. Aisha brought her toys and dolls with her. Muhammad consummated the union to the little girl within hours. Readers may form their own opinions about his conduct.

Gabriel had brought a message from Allah that Muslims could take only four wives but when Muhammad already had four wives he found an attractive widow named Umm Salamah. Gabriel then helpfully brought another message from Allah to Muhammad that he alone amongst Muslims could take as many wives as he wished and he ended up with twelve wives. The practise of very controlling religious leaders taking multiple "wives" has been repeated in more recent times among Mormons and some other Christian sects in America.

When Muhammad and his Muslim followers first arrived at the beautiful green oases of Medina three Jewish tribes had already been long established there. They were the Beni Qaynuqa, the Beni Nadir and the Beni Qurayzah, secure within their own mud walled fortified villages. The firm belief of these Jews in their ancient faith constantly undermined Muhammad's mystical accounts of his revelations. In due course Muhammad found reasons to besiege and destroy them one by one. The Muslims, not having military assault weapons, blockaded each village in turn and starved it into submission.

The first was the village of the Beni Qaynuqa whose lives were spared but all their land, goods, livestock, armour and homes were confiscated.

The second was the village of the Beni Nadir whose armour and fixed property was seized but they were allowed to keep all their portable possessions and livestock. They decided to leave Medina in style with their women in all their jewels and finery to the sound of music, drums and singing.

The third village was that of the Beni Qurayzah which was not so fortunate. It had sided with the Meccans in a previous encounter against the Muslims. The Beni Qurayzah surrendered unconditionally. All the eight hundred men of the Beni Qurayzah had their hands tied behind their backs. When they would not convert to Islam, they were taken out in small groups and beheaded one by one. The men's bodies were thrown in a ditch and all their women and children were sold into slavery. This act of ruthless genocide sent shockwaves throughout Arabia and the Middle East. It is difficult to understand the guidance from the God of Abraham to his Apostle Muhammad for this treatment of His most faithful Chosen People. The pagan Arabs of Arabia were not particularly religious and they got the message that to resist Islam could mean total annihilation, so in future they took the safe option of conversion to Islam.

THE BELIEFS OF MUSLIMS

Muhammad introduced rules for the virtues of equality, generosity and hospitality to be observed by his followers within the community of believers.

Islam, as defined in the Koran, largely agrees with, updates and expands the information in the Old and New Testaments of the Christian Bible. The main tenets of Islam are that there is one God, the source of creation who disposes all lives and events. Muhammad is God's messenger. All people should become one community and on the Day of Judgement all living and dead will arise, be judged and sent to the joys of Heaven or the tortures of Hell forever.

The five requirements of the Islamic faith are:

1.   Declaration of faith.
2.   Prayer (5 times per day).
3.   Giving alms for the poor.
4.   Pilgrimage to Mecca (at least once if affordable).
5.   Daylight fasting during the lunar month of Ramadan.

The Koran is the Islamic Holy book of God's instructions to mankind as passed by the Archangel Gabriel to Muhammad, heard as a voice in Muhammad's head. Some Muslims do not believe in democracy because they claim to live by Allah's laws as revealed in the Koran, not by men's laws as invented in Parliaments or Assemblies. As in the Bible, the Koran has instructions to love God with all your might and to love your neighbour as yourself. Jews and Christians can be tolerated but must be taxed. The Koran orders modest clothing for women on Earth, but provides a well stocked Alfresco Bordello for men in Heaven. Just like the Bible the Koran contains many contradictions. Kindly verses requiring generosity and helpfulness are contradicted by other sample verses below:

"*Allah's curse is on the infidels!*" (2:86).

"*Allah is the enemy of the infidels!*" (2:98).

"*Unbelievers shall have woeful punishment!*" 2:175).

"*Slay unbelievers where you find them…put them to the sword!*" (2:190-193).

"*We will put terror into the hearts of the unbelievers!*" (3:149-151).

Can there ever be peace in the world while thousands of boys are being taught in Muslim religious schools that it is a religious duty to kill all people who have other beliefs?

It is very difficult to get Muslims to reconsider their beliefs because if they should decide to give up their beliefs they must be killed by other Muslims.

It must not be assumed from the above that all Muslims are violent Jihadis. Most Muslims are generous and hospitable people who choose to follow the alternative peace loving verses of the Koran.

IS THE SPEAKER TRUSTWORTHY?

With regard to the Founders of the three Middle Eastern faiths, the information on their behaviour and their psychotic mental health comes directly recorded from the Bible, the Koran and the Hadiths. It is therefore worth giving time to ponder some questions, including for example:-

- *Should Abraham, who lied and prostituted his wife for profit, be trusted and believed?*

- *Should Jesus Christ, who said he saw and talked to the Devil and whose twelve chosen companions were specially picked by him because they hated their own families, be trusted and believed?*

- *Should Muhammad, who said he got messages from the Angel Gabriel, flew to Heaven on a winged horse and who ordered mass slaughter of Jews, be trusted and believed?*

THE THREE RELIGIONS OF INDIA

The three great religions of India are Hinduism, Buddhism and Sikhism. All three have been tolerant of other faiths and all three encompass the idea of repeated reincarnations of the soul. Hinduism is the most ancient of all existing religions, its earliest origins are lost in the mists of time.

Hindus generally have at heart the idea that all religious believers in God are Hindus in other forms. Other religions use different names for God and different forms of worship. Hindus themselves have many names for God and many forms of worship so other ideas of this sort were perfectly acceptable to them. The concept of heresy or of punishing others for worshiping god in different ways is quite unthinkable to the Hindu mind.

Buddhism was developed through meditation by Siddhartha Gautama around 500BC. He had been brought up as a Hindu. Buddhism has no Gods but it has "belief in a superhuman controlling power" that gives justice by reincarnation and so it qualifies as a religion under the Oxford dictionary definition.

Sikhism is the most modern of the world's great religions. It originated with the thoughts developed through meditation by Guru Nanak (1469-1539) who was born to Hindu parents in the Punjab. Sikhism had the advantage of incorporating some better aspects of older religions and adding some wise new ideas.

THE ORIGINS OF HINDUISM

Hindu sacred texts are the most ancient religious texts surviving to the present, indeed they are probably the oldest form of written records that have remained in continuous use up to the present. In oral form some are probably over 4,000 years old and they have existed in Sanskrit written form from at least 500BC.

The Hindu sacred texts of the Rig Veda, Sama Veda, Yajur Veda, and Atharva Vedas, they contain hymns, incantations, and rituals from ancient India. The Upanishads deal with Vedic philosophy and form the conclusions of each of the Vedas. They elaborate on how the soul (Atman) can be united with the ultimate truth (Brahman) through contemplation and meditation, as well as the doctrine of Kharma – which is the cumulative effect of a person's actions.

An important ancient text is the Ramayana. It is a moving love story with moral and spiritual themes, it has deep appeal in India. It concerns the exploits of the hero Rama who is viewed as an incarnation of the god Vishnu.

The Mahabharata is a group of books relating legends and its sixth book is the Bhagavad Gita which is particularly popular and honoured for its insight into duty and ethics. It is related as a conversation on a battlefield between the warrior Arjuna and the God Krishna. There are many more sacred Hindu texts which include the Brahmanas, Sutras, Puranas, Aranyakas, etc.

THE BELIEFS OF HINDUS

There is one God Brahma who can take many male and female forms.

Principally, Brahma is the Creator of the Universe.

Vishnu, (Krishna) is the Preserver, who is responsible for righteousness, eternal order, religion, law and duty.

Shiva, is the Destroyer who is at times compassionate, erotic or destructive.

Lakshmi, Goddess and consort of Vishnu, represents wealth and purity.

Many other Goddess forms and incarnations include Parvati, Durga, Kali and others.

Hindus believe in repeated transmigrations of the soul resulting in being reborn into better or worse circumstances in the next life depending on behaviour in the previous life. Escape from this cycle is believed possible by meditation and virtuous conduct. The lofty ideals of Hinduism are detracted by the ancient customs of the caste system whereby people are supposed to remain in the social group into which they were born; Priests, soldiers, merchants, farmers, labourers, outcasts etc. Caste customs were probably invented about 3,000 years ago to stabilise society. Some Caste customs remain today in spite of the Indian Government's efforts to ameliorate or eradicate them. In recent years, there have been some disturbing developments. Attacks by Hindu extremists have taken place on the Babri Masjid mosque at Ayodhya and on Christian churches in the states of Orissa and Chattisgarh. The most peaceful and gentle adherents of Hinduism are the vegetarian Jains who have a noble discipline of never harming any form of life that can feel suffering.

Ideally, Hindus are guided by four main aims:-

Dharma: *Righteousness in living.*

Artha: *Pursuit of material prosperity.*

Kama: *Pleasure, whether mental or sensual.*

Moksa: *Ultimate liberation by renouncement of the world.*

THE ORIGINS OF BUDDHISM

Siddhartha Gautama was the son of a Hindu prince. He was born about 500BC in the village of Lumbini in southern Nepal. After marriage and having fathered a son in a privileged and sheltered life, he was shocked to discover the hardships and injustices outside in the real world at large. Seeking to make sense of the injustice of these ugly realities, he chose a life of wandering self-denial and through meditation he achieved understanding, called "Enlightenment", and became known as the Buddha (Wise One).

The original teachings of the Buddha are philosophical and analytical guides to spiritual development they are pure moral philosophy and cannot qualify as religion under the Oxford dictionary definition of religion because they do not include "Belief in a superhuman controlling power".

There are, however, later developments of Buddhism that incorporate the idea of reincarnation. Some of these later developments of Buddhism qualify as religion because they include belief in a superhuman controlling power that arranges for the transfer of the soul after death into a newborn infant that is born into better or worse circumstances as deserved by the soul's living behaviour in its previous life.

THE BELIEFS OF BUDDHISTS

Although the idea of reincarnation is not mentioned in the original Buddhist scriptures, nevertheless, some Buddhists believe in repetitious transmigrations of the soul as believed by the Hindus and Sikhs.

The Buddha taught that there are Four Noble Truths of human existence:

1.   Dukkha: Life involves sorrow and suffering.
2.   Samudaya: Suffering is due to craving wrong things or having wrong ideas.
3.   Nirodha: It is possible to find an end to suffering.
4.   Marga: The Way to the end of suffering is The Noble Eightfold Path.

The Eightfold Path comprises personal acquisition of these attributes:

1.   Right Views
2.   Right Intention
3.   Right Speech
4.   Right Action
5.   Right Livelihood
6.   Right Effort
7.   Right Mindfulness
8.   Right Concentration

Each of these eight instructions is expanded with explanation of the thoughts, actions, intentions, wisdom, ethics and mental development required.

Although the beautiful idea of some form of superhuman justice is comforting, there is no evidence to show that there is any truth in reincarnation, just as there is no evidence for any superhuman controlling power.

THE ORIGINS OF SIKHISM

The inspired man who created the Sikh religion was Guru Nanak (1469-1539). He was born in the Punjab of northern India and was the first of ten individual men (Gurus) who led the Sikh faith. The tenth and last was Guru Gobind Singh Ji.

The Sikhs had suffered such religious intolerance and awful atrocities at the hands of the Muslim Mogul Emperor's authorities over the centuries that Guru Gobind determined in 1708 that there would be no more living Gurus to lead the religion.

In future the religion would be led by the ideas in its Holy Book the "Guru Granth Sahib". The book was given a man's name and is given the respect and honour of the leader. Guru Gobind wisely knew that the ideas in the book could be copied thousands of times. He knew that ideas can never be killed nor tortured nor its innocent children executed as had happened to his own children and to past Gurus. Guru Gobind, in making this decision also made provision for unknown circumstances of the future so that the Holy Book would not become fixed in the past (like the Torah, Bible or Koran). Guru Gobind recommended that, if future occasions arose that were not covered by words in the Guru Granth Sahib, the Sikh community could agree new words under its guiding thoughts.

THE BELIEFS OF SIKHS

Sikhs stress the importance of good actions over rituals.
Sikhs believe that they should ideally follow these instructions:

1.   Keep God in heart and mind at all times.
2.   Live honestly and work hard.
3.   Treat everyone equally.
4.   Be generous to the less fortunate.
5.   Serve others.

The Sikh temples of worship are called Gurdwaras, people of all faiths or none are made welcome inside. Many Sikh men wear turbans for identity.

Sikhs believe in:

- Freedom of speech and religion.
- Justice and liberty for all.
- Defending civil liberties and protecting the defenceless.
- Tolerance and equality, regardless of gender, caste, race or religion.
- One God in common for all humanity.
- Equal rights for women.

Sikhs do NOT believe in:

- Terrorism or hurting the innocent.
- Race hate or racial profiling.
- Any war based on religion.
- Trying to convert others to their Faith.
- Fasting.

As with all other religions, existence of God is not supported by any evidence, (Author).

CONCLUSIONS

If one looks at the sky on a clear night with a telescope countless billions of stars and galaxies can be seen. Purely by chance the conditions for life to begin will exist somewhere in the Universe as we know we have them here.

- If a planet is too near its sun it will be too hot, (water boils).
- If it is too far from its sun it will be too cold, (water freezes).
- If it is too small it will not have enough gravity to hold an atmosphere.
- If it is too big its gravity holds so much gas that light will not reach the surface.
- If it is not spinning it will not generate magnetism to deflect deadly solar and interstellar particles.
- If it has no moon orbiting it, the planet's axis of rotation may move until it is pointing toward its sun so that half is in permanent scorched day and the other half in permanent frozen night.

The conditions for life to evolve can exist by pure chance from the billions of cosmic possibilities without any reason for an imaginary Creator.

Palaeontologists tell us that fossil records indicate that 98% of all the creatures that have ever lived are now extinct. One day in the distant future we humans too will join the long list of the extinct. The moral of this is that we should do what we can to make life pleasant for all in the millennia of time that remains for us.

Because we plan purposefully as individuals, to support our families and achieve our aims, we tend to have an instinctive assumption that all existence is for a planned purpose. Because we usually have a reason for doing things we tend to have an instinctive assumption that there must be some reason for everything. These two assumptions have no basis in logic and they support an arrogant self-importance and pride that humans are specially chosen and more than just clever monkeys. Other subconscious conditioning from childhood lies in the continued immature assumption of an all powerful parent figure into adulthood. The biological instinct for survival that makes us avoid injury or death is also the cause of a survival wish for life after death.

The choice of which religion, if any, should be followed is almost invariably devoid of intellectual input. Attempts to consider which of the many dead religions of the past should be chosen or which of the six religions of the present should be chosen to follow are rare. The simple fact is that most religious people just follow the customs of their family or society without the application of any reasoning and they then assume that what is heard first is exclusive absolute truth. This conditioning is very easily passed on to innocent children who are generally unable to resist this mental imprint.

Consideration should be given to the serious clinical psychotic personality disorders experienced by the three Founders of the Middle Eastern religions. These three Founders are discredited by their personal behaviour and the hallucinations that make their accounts of supernatural experiences unbelievable. The hallucinating mental disorder of "Voices in the Head" gave these three Founders exceptional self-confidence due to their arrogant belief that they had been personally chosen by an Almighty God. This self-confidence was further reinforced when they found themselves believed and supported by uneducated and gullible listeners. The success of these Founders was also helped by the instinctive need of inexperienced and indecisive people to find and follow a convincing and confident leader.

The sublime beauty of some religious art, architecture and music is not evidence for supernatural phenomena.

Generosity, truth, justice, kindness, tolerance, and all forms of good behaviour are not dependent upon religion.

Religions only exist because some people without proof or evidence pass to uneducated or primitive folk the thought that imaginary supernatural ideas are real and true. Additionally, without proof or evidence, some adults persuade children that superhuman controlling powers really exist. Were it not for these misleading abuses of innocent minds, religions, religious wars and their associated terrorisms would not exist.

It is awkward for Christian politicians and leaders to criticise the beliefs of Islamic terrorists when they hold equally irrational beliefs themselves. The effect of religion on world conflict and politics remains profound. For example, the Queen of the United Kingdom is Head of the Anglican Church of England. Anglican bishops are appointed to the legislature in the House of Lords. American Christians elect Christian politicians. Jews believe God gave Palestine to the Jews. Muslims believe Allah gave the world to one world community of Muslims. American politicians support the Jews in Israel/Palestine because they believe their God gave the land to Abraham and his Jews. The inhabitants fight over the land thinking they obey God's wishes.

Irrational religious beliefs can rarely be successfully countered with rational arguments or logical points of view. However, irrational beliefs can be successfully dismissed with ridicule and mockery.

It is easy for most people just to go along with surrounding customs and beliefs without engaging any intellectual effort of enquiry. They just allow themselves, without any rational application of logic, to become convinced that opinions commonly heard around them represent absolute truths. This attitude resulted in the mass murder and suicides of 909 followers and their children at the Reverend Jim Jones'

People's Temple at Jonestown, Guyana in 1978. In other cases this attitude sometimes results in the recruitment of terrorist suicide bombers.

Religious faith can be a great comfort to some believers. It can be an unworldly powerful sensation. Religious Faith exists entirely in an imaginary world outside the real world. In the real world upholding civilisation there is hopefully systematic reliance on truth through evidence by all responsible people such as, scientists, engineers, doctors, lawyers and police.

Glenn Francis Hill, January 2012.

BIBLIOGRAPHY

Abdullah Yusuf Ali: *The Holy Qur'an,* Islamic Propagation Centre, 1946.

Armstrong, Karen: *Muhammad, a Prophet for our Time,* Harper Press, 2006.

Ayer, Sir Alfred: *Language, Truth and Logic,* Penguin Books, 1971.

Bentall, Richard: *Madness Explained,* Allen Lane, 2003.

Blackburn, Simon: *Oxford Dictionary of Philosophy,* Oxford Univ. Press, 1994.

Burleigh, Michael: *Sacred Causes,* Harper Press, 2006.

Colman, Andrew: *Oxford Dictionary of Psychology,* Oxford Univ. Press, 2004.

Czerner, Thomas B, *What makes you Tick,* John Wiley & Sons, 2001.

Dawkins, Richard: *The God Delusion,* Transworld Publishers, 2006.

De Rosa, Peter: *Vicars of Christ, the Dark Side of the Papacy,* Corgi Books, 1989.

Fisk, Robert: *The Great War for Civilisation,* Harper Perennial, 2006.

Frazer, Sir James: *The Golden Bough,* Wordsworth Editions, 1993.

Gibbon, Edward: *Decline & Fall of the Roman Empire,* Chatto & Windus, 1960.

Gilbert, Martin: *Israel a History,* Doubleday,1998

Glubb, Sir John Bagot: *Life& Times of Muhammad,* Hodder & Stoughton, 1970.

Harris, Sam: *The End of Faith,* Simon & Schuster, 2005.

Harris, Sam: *Letter to a Christian Nation,* Transworld Publishers, 2007.

Humphrys, John: *In God We Doubt,* Hodder & Stoughton, 2007.

Hume, David: *An Enquiry concerning Human Understanding,* Oxford World Classics, 2007.

King James Version: *Holy Bible,* Cambridge University Press, 2002.

Josephus, Flavius: *The Jewish War,* Penguin Classics, 1959.

Larousse, *Encyclopedia of Mythology*, Hamlyn Publishing, 1968.

Magnusson, Magnus: *Chambers Biographical Dictionary,* 1990.

Nokes, David: *Jonathan Swift,* Oxford University Press, 1985.

McGreal, Ian P: *Great Thinkers of the Eastern World,* Harper Collins, 1995.

Pappe, Ilan: *The Ethnic Cleansing of Palestine,* Oneworld Publications, 2006.

Rogerson, Barnaby: *The Prophet Muhammad,* Little, Brown, 2003.

Rose, Norman: *Chaim Weizmann, a biography,* Weidenfelt & Nicholson, 1986.

Roy, Olivier: *Secularism Confronts Islam,* Columbia University Press, 2007.

Russell, Lord Bertrand: *Why I am not a Christian,* Watts & Co., London, 1927.

Smith, Sir William: *Smaller Dictionary of the Bible,* John Murray, 1907.

Shri Purohit Swami: *The Geeta,* Faber & Faber Ltd. London, 1935.

Taylor, A.J.P: *Lloyd George,* Cambridge UniversityPress,1961.

Wood, Ernest: *Yoga,* Cassell & Co., London, 1959.